# better together

**This book is best read together, grownup and kid.**

akidsco.com

a kids book about

# a kids book about CHEMOTHERAPY

by Maeve Clinton

# a kids book about

Text and design copyright © 2023
by A Kids Book About, Inc.

Copyright is good! It ensures that work like this can exist, and more work in the future can be created.

All rights reserved. No part of this publication may be reproduced, distributed, or transmitted in any form or by any means, including photocopying, recording, other electronic or mechanical methods, without the prior written permission of the publisher, except in the case of brief quotations embodied in critical reviews and certain other noncommercial uses permitted by copyright law. For permission requests, write to the publisher.

A Kids Book About, Kids Are Ready, and the colophon 'a' are trademarks of A Kids Book About, Inc.

Printed in the United States of America.

A Kids Book About books are available online: *akidsco.com*

To share your stories, ask questions, or inquire about bulk purchases (schools, libraries, and nonprofits), please use the following email address: *hello@akidsco.com*

Print ISBN: 978-1-958825-69-3
Ebook ISBN: 978-1-958825-70-9

Designed by Rick DeLucco
Edited by Emma Wolf

To my mom, Carol Clinton, an ovarian cancer warrior. I love you and I miss you.

# Intro

When my mom started going through chemotherapy, it was scary for me. It probably feels scary for you too. How will you talk to your kid? How will you explain how it works? Will they understand?

It's not easy. There are so many changes happening and all so quickly. Topics like cancer and chemotherapy feel big and difficult to talk about. It can be hard to know where to start when diving into these conversations. But in reading this book, you're doing the most important thing: opening the door for kids to understand what is going on in the world around them.

My hope is this book will give you and your kid the chance to have open and honest conversations about the treatment their person is or will be going through. By giving kids the chance to learn more and ask questions, you'll also have the opportunity to share how to cope and move forward through this difficult time, together.

Hi, my name is **Maeve.**

When I was 5, my mom was diagnosed with ovarian cancer.

Because of that, she started
going through something called

→ **CHEMOTHERAPY.**

The whole process was really confusing to me, and grownups had a hard time explaining it.

I wrote this book to help kids like you understand what it means when someone gets chemotherapy.

# CHEMOTHERAPY IS A TREATMENT FOR CANCER.

There are other ways to treat cancer; chemotherapy is just one of them.

Chemotherapy is a big word.
Sometimes people just call it "chemo."

So, how does it work?

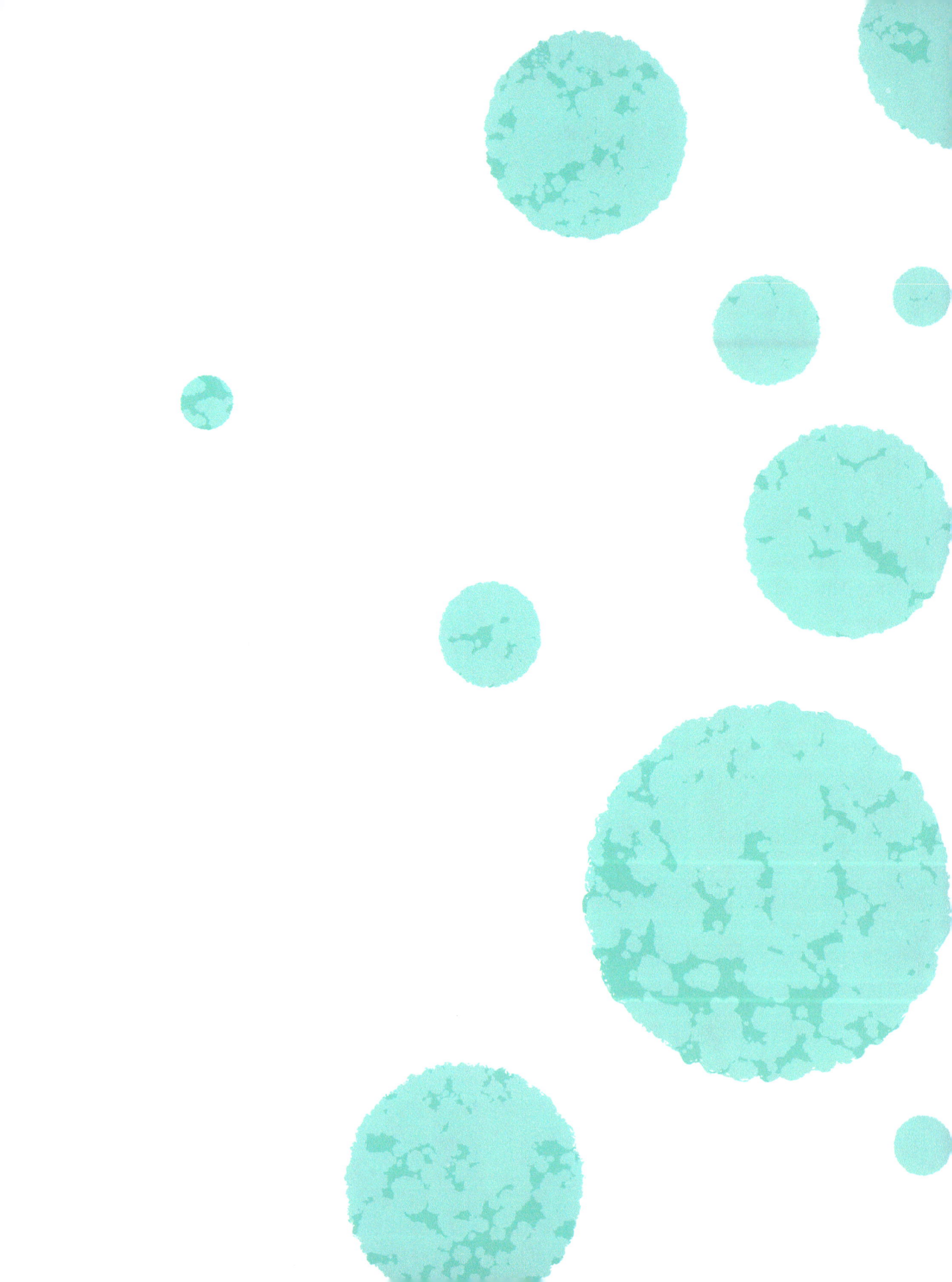

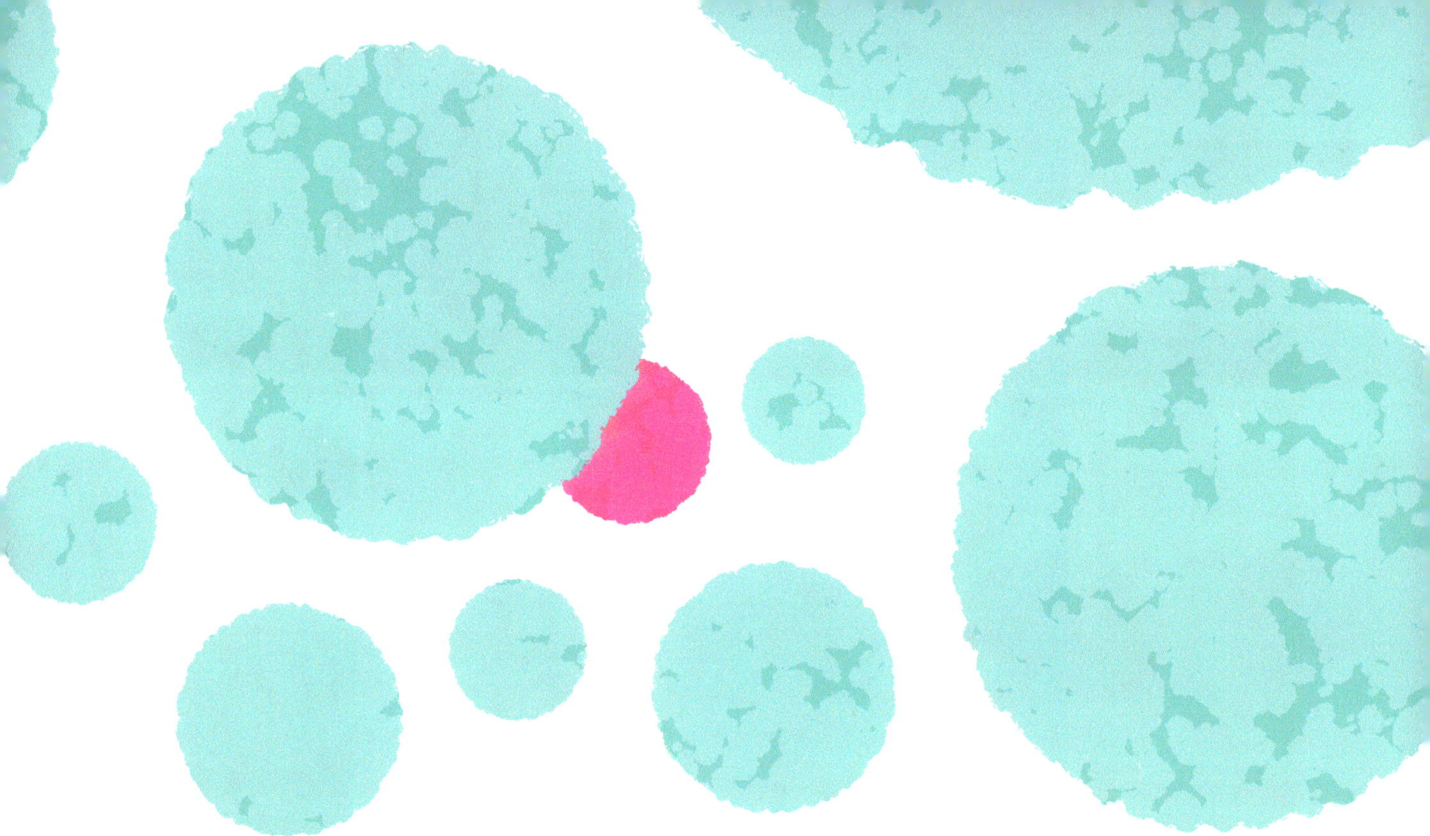

All human beings are made of cells.

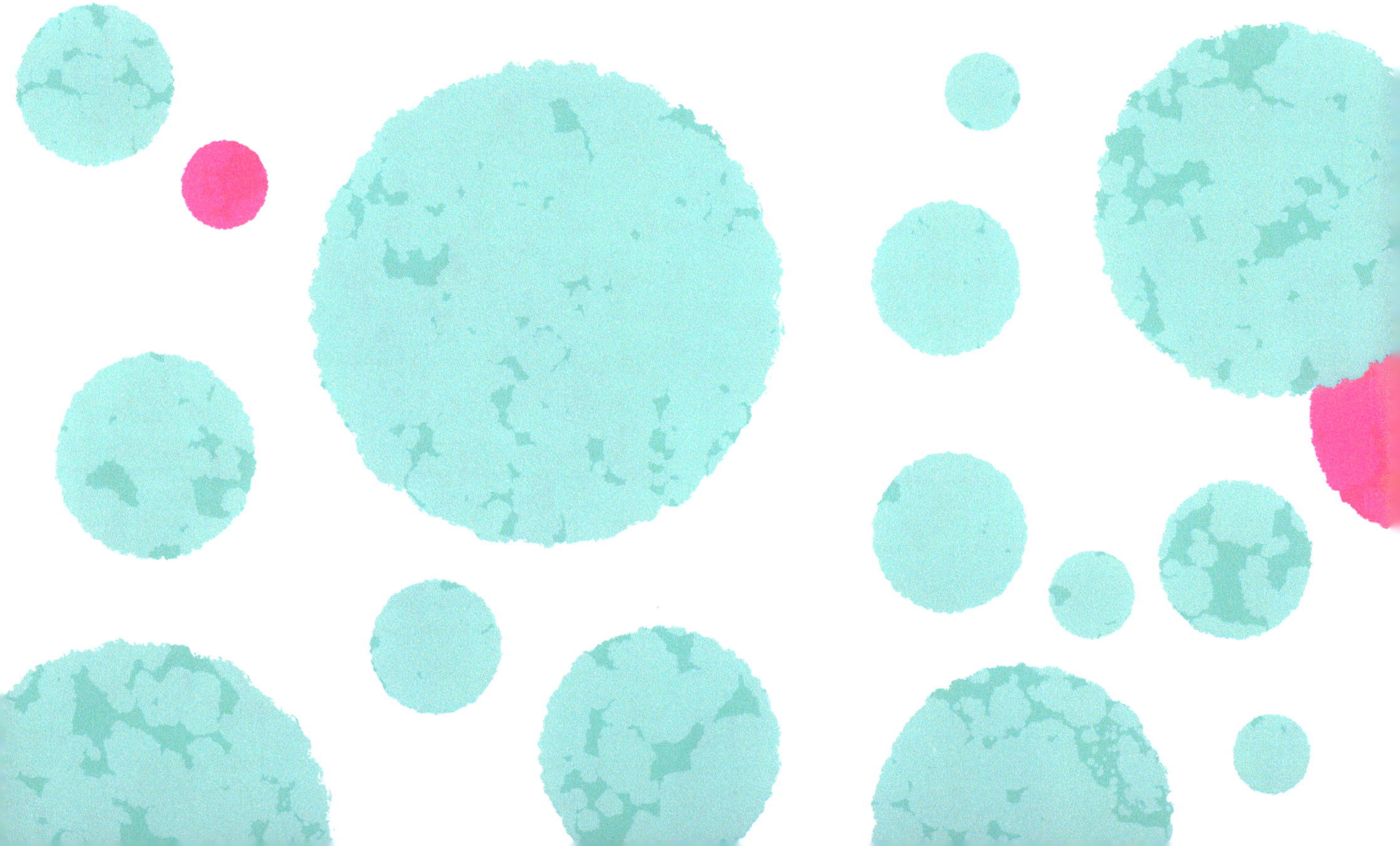

People who are diagnosed with cancer have cells in their bodies that make them sick.

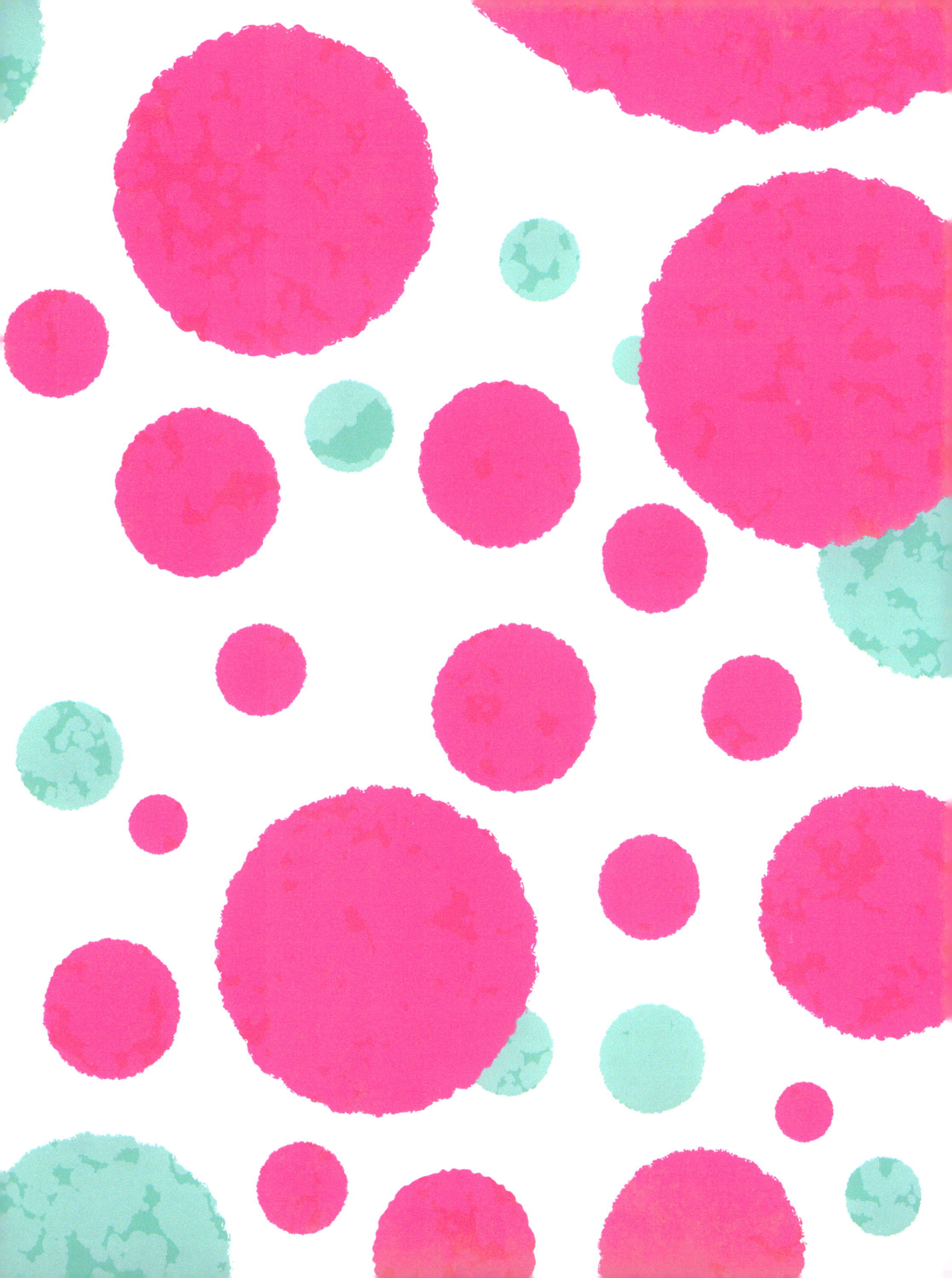

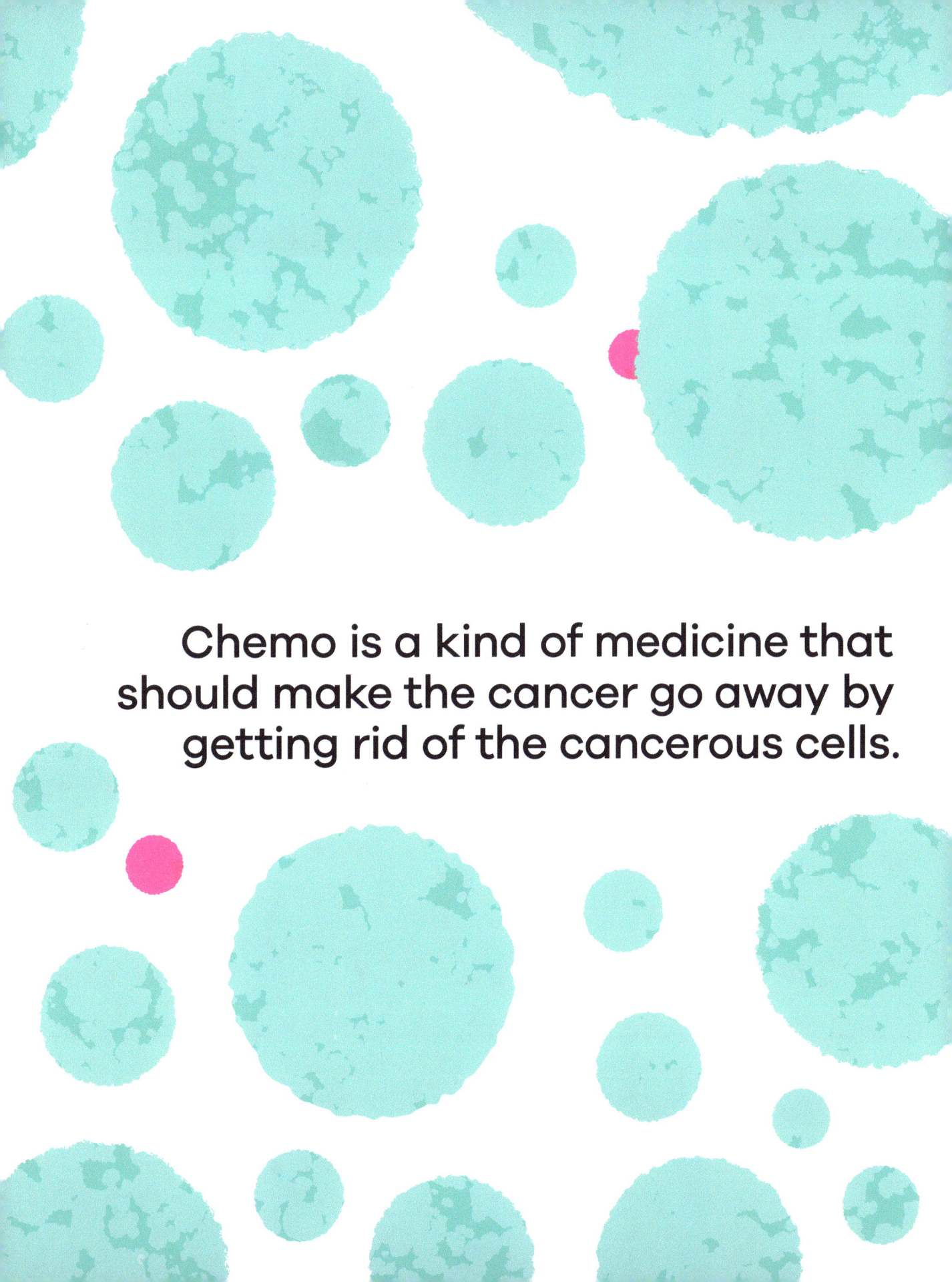

Chemo is a kind of medicine that should make the cancer go away by getting rid of the cancerous cells.

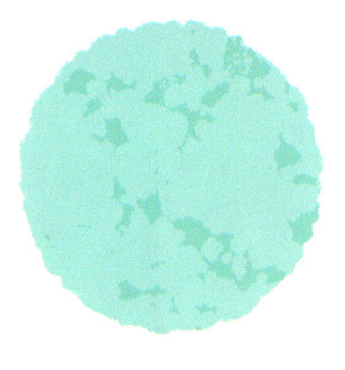

When someone gets chemo, they go to the doctor's office more often.

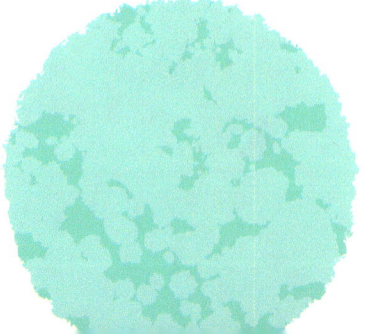

They might go every week, once a month, or however frequently their doctor thinks is best based on their diagnosis.

# CHEMOTHERAPY CAN BE DONE

IN SEVERAL DIFFERENT WAYS.

When my mom went through chemo, she went to the doctor once a week.

When she was there, she sat in a chair and a nurse put an IV\* in her arm that carried the medicine to her body.

\*An IV carries a kind of medicine from outside the body into it through a person's veins. "IV" stands for "intravenous," which means "in the vein."

When people are receiving chemotherapy, they will be able to stay awake, but they might get sleepy and need a nap.

Or they might:

Chemo can last 1 to 7 hours, or even a couple of days—it is different for every person.

However long it lasts, the doctors and nurses will take really good care of your person while they're going through it.

I remember that, during the day, it was hard not to worry about my mom in chemo.

But continuing with my daily activities helped me focus on something else.

While your loved one is getting chemo, you might still go to school, or a friend's house, or to soccer practice.

You're still allowed to

# HAVE FUN

and

# BE A KID!

When they come home
from chemotherapy,
they might feel really tired. zzzzzzzzzz

ZZZZZZZZZZZZ

You can write them notes while they are taking a nap to tell them about your day and let them know you love them!

My siblings and I used to write notes for my mom, and she kept every single one of them.

# AFTER A COUPLE OF WEEKS OF CHEMO...

your person might
start to lose their hair,
or their belly might hurt,
or they might be really
tired because their body
is working so hard to get
rid of the cancer cells.

Seeing my mom lose her hair was really scary for me.

But these are common side effects for someone going through chemotherapy.

It just means they are getting the medicine they need.

**Physically, it can seem like your person is going through a lot of changes.**

BUT THEY STILL LOVE
YOU JUST THE SAME.

IT'S **OK** TO FEEL
OR WORRIED—
YOU'RE FEELING

# SCARED ANYTHING IS NORMAL.

You can talk about how you feel with a safe grownup like:

a parent,

aunt,

uncle,

grandparent,

teacher,

therapist,

coach,

or someone who is trustworthy.

It's also normal to have a ton of questions. I know I had a lot when I was a kid.

Questions like...

IS MY MOM SCARED?

WHAT IS HER DOCTOR'S NAME?

WILL SHE ALWAYS HAVE TO GET CHEMOTHERAPY?

WHAT CAN I DO TO HELP?

You're allowed to ask questions, too.

**What's on your mind?**

Turn to the grownup reading this with you and share what you've been wondering about. I'll wait!

I'm so proud of you for

# BEING

# BRAVE

even though it probably feels scary.

If you're ready,
# GIVE YOUR PERSON A BIG HUG

AND TELL THEM YOU LOVE THEM.

YOUR PERSON LOVES YOU SO SO KEEP BEING

MUCH.
YOU.

# Outro

OK, take a deep breath! Starting the conversation is the hardest part, but now the door is open for you and your kid to talk. Being vulnerable can go a long way, and it will make all the difference for your kid. You can show that even though you feel sad, you choose to use healthy coping skills and remain as positive as possible. The best way to teach your kid to be brave is by being brave yourself.

I hope you'll revisit this book whenever you need to reopen the discussion, or if you need to share new information, or if your kid has new questions. Thank you for being brave. I am proud of you.

# About The Author

Maeve Clinton (she/her) wrote this book to help parents navigate difficult conversations about people going through chemotherapy. Maeve's mom, Carol Clinton, was diagnosed with stage 3 advanced ovarian cancer when Maeve was 5 years old.

Throughout her life, Maeve has been passionate about helping other people. She is now a licensed social worker and works as a children's therapist.

When she thinks back to being young and having a parent going through cancer treatment, she wishes her grownups would have had kid-friendly resources to help start tough conversations.

Maeve's hope is that you'll talk with your kids, give kids the opportunity to ask questions, and be open and vulnerable about how you're feeling, too.

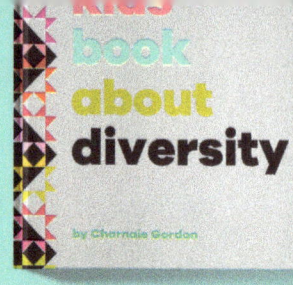

Discover more at **akidsco.com**

www.ingramcontent.com/pod-product-compliance
Lightning Source LLC
Chambersburg PA
CBHW061359010526
44107CB00012B/983